Ways Animals Sleep

A spotted fawn has curled up for a rest among rocks and leaves.

by Jane R. McCauley

☐ BOOKS FOR YOUNG EXPLORERS
☐ NATIONAL GEOGRAPHIC SOCIETY

COPYRIGHT © 1983 NATIONAL GEOGRAPHIC SOCIETY   LIBRARY OF CONGRESS ℭℐℙ DATA P. 32

Shhh! In a cool, shady cave, a mountain lion mother is napping with her cubs close beside her. A cave makes a safe home for them.

Just like you, all animals need some form of rest every day. Most animals have a special place where they sleep, but some just curl up on the ground. Some sleep floating in the water. Others find safe places to sleep in the trees. Wherever they are, animals have ways of protecting themselves while they sleep.

On a warm day, a family
of raccoons naps in a tree.
Baby raccoons, called cubs,
are born in the spring.
While they grow, young
animals need to sleep a lot.
How cozy this furry bundle
of tiny cubs looks!

A mother raccoon watches
over her cubs in their den
in a hollow tree stump.
The cubs stay close to her
when they are young.

Sometimes many animals crowd together to sleep. Walruses usually live in large herds in the icy waters of the far north. From time to time, they gather on rocky shores and rest.

This walrus is sleeping on its side. You can see its front teeth, or tusks. By fanning its flipper in the air, a walrus stays cool in the warm sun.

It seems hard for walruses to rest. They are always sniffing and snorting. When one turns over, it wakes up another and another and another.

Sea lions can sleep floating in the ocean, with one flipper up.
The flipper soaks up sunshine and helps keep the animal warm.
Sea lions hold their heads out of the water to breathe.

A sea otter is resting on its back in a bed of kelp, a kind of seaweed. Roots of the kelp are attached to the seafloor. With the kelp pulled over its body, the otter will not drift away.

Upside down, an animal called a manatee naps underwater. Soon it will rise to the surface for air.

Seals can sleep on land or underwater. This gray seal slowly bobs up and down as it rests on the surface. Air in the seal's body helps it keep its nose above water. Thick layers of fat around its body also help it stay afloat.

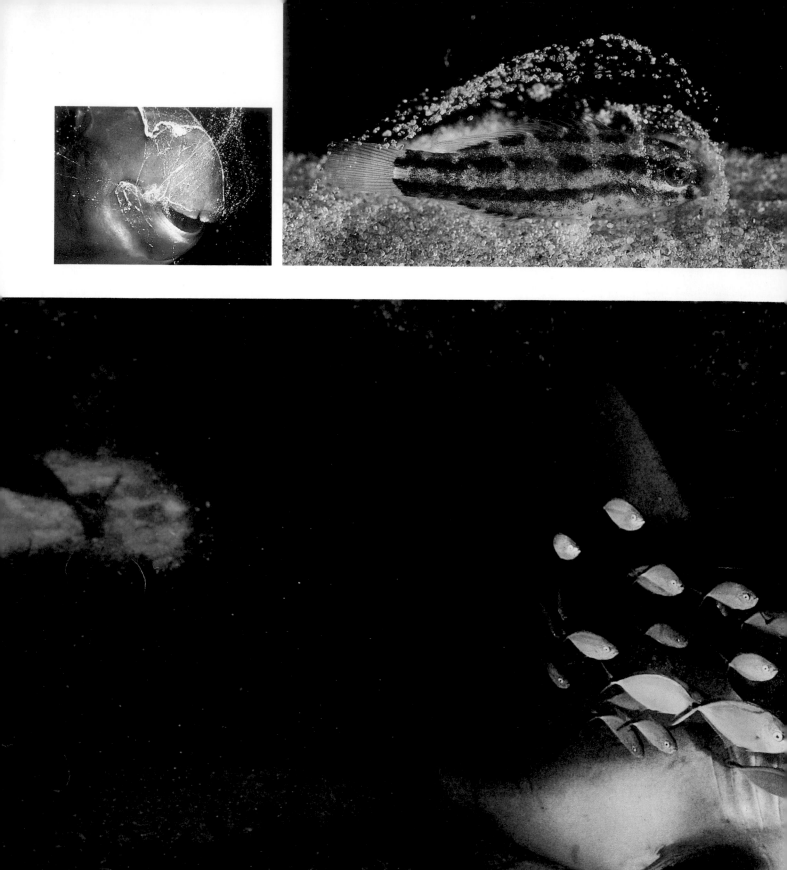

Unlike you, fish can never close their eyes. They have no eyelids. This shark, a kind of fish, lies very still in an underwater cave.

Look at the mouth of the parrotfish. Do you see the jellylike bubble the fish is blowing around itself? Inside the bubble, the parrotfish is safe from larger fish while it rests through the night.

All in a row, these ducks are getting ready for a nap. Like many birds, ducks rest on one leg with their bills tucked under their feathers. Which duck do you think is already asleep?

Some birds sleep during the day, but they have ways of staying safe while resting. Up in a tree, this young screech owl has shut its eyes. It cannot fall because its claws lock tightly around a branch. A dark-colored whippoorwill sitting on a log is hard to see in the daylight. With its long neck twisted around, a swan sleeps on the water.

Many animals sleep in trees, where they can be safe. Others, like this leopard, find cool shade there on a hot day. A furry koala is snuggling between high branches. It will sleep there most of the day.

A young male orangutan lies on his back in his nest. He wraps his fingers and toes around tree branches. Nearly every night, orangutans make new leafy beds.

When cold weather comes, most bears go into dens and sleep. Sometimes they wake up and yawn and look around. Their winter sleep is one kind of hibernation. Bear cubs are born in winter. By early spring, they are ready to go out in the bright sunshine with their mother.

The young cubs like to play. But while their mother naps, they will not leave her side.

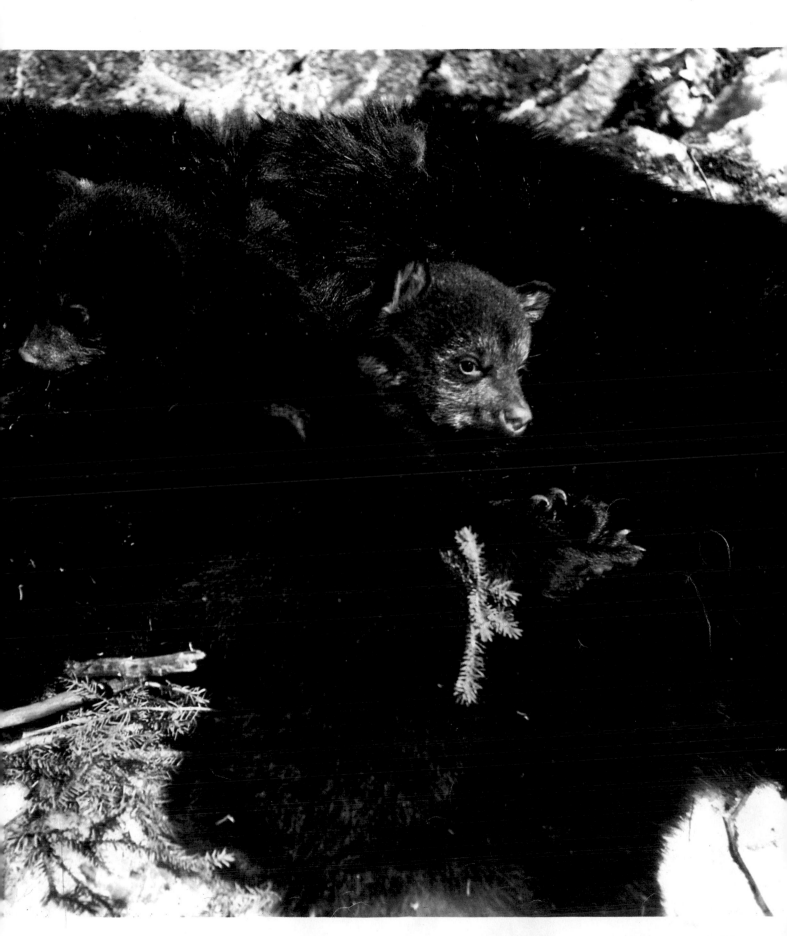

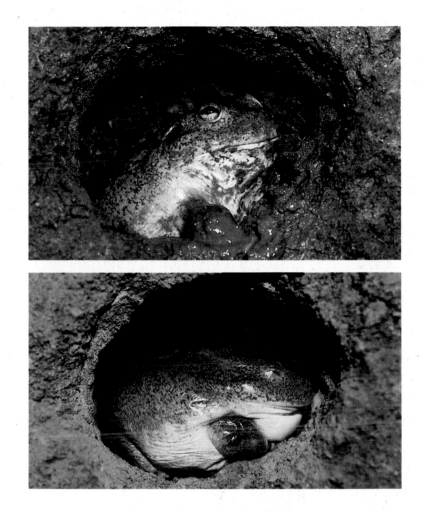

When a chipmunk hibernates, it curls into a furry ball underground. Now and then, the animal wakes up and nibbles on food it stored in its nest.

This frog digs a hole in the mud as the desert becomes hot and dry. The frog may lie in its hole for months. During this time, a covering of old skin helps keep the frog moist as it sleeps. Its special rest is called aestivation.

Insects stay busy most of the time, but they, too, must rest. One rainy night a katydid rests under a leaf that makes a good umbrella. Don't you think the green, upside-down katydid looks like part of the plant?

In the cooler temperature of evening, it is hard for bees to keep moving. A group of bees has slowed down for the night. They hold on to a plant with their tiny jaws. Another bee crawls from a flower, where it rested overnight.

Light frost covers a
damselfly that stopped
on a bush to rest.
The warm sun will
melt the frost. Then
the insect can fly away.

A busy prairie dog carries a bunch of grass into its burrow. Prairie dogs usually sleep in their underground homes. After a big meal, though, this one is so sleepy it sits right down outside. In the warm sunshine, it grows sleepier . . . and sleepier. Soon, it will scurry into its home.

Male bighorn sheep, called rams, rest on a mountainside. They live in the open, where their enemies might easily catch them. The rams will not stay asleep for long. This is one way they protect themselves.

This ram has settled down on the ground and closed his eyes. While he takes it easy, he sniffs the air and listens for danger. He can wake up very quickly. Bighorns nap for a shorter time than it takes you to climb into bed, but they rest often during the day.

Hares, too, take many short naps, but they stay alert. This hare is ready to hop away if an enemy comes near.

Lions can sleep many hours a day. A group of lions, called a pride, is lying in the shade. Face to face, two males share a branch for a pillow.

Animals lead busy lives. Like you, they need to sleep so their bodies can store up energy for all the different things they do. When you go to bed tonight, think about all the animals around you. Perhaps they are already fast asleep.

Published by The National Geographic Society
Gilbert M. Grosvenor, *President;* Melvin M. Payne, *Chairman of the Board;*
Owen R. Anderson, *Executive Vice President;* Robert L. Breeden, *Vice President,*
Publications and Educational Media

Prepared by The Special Publications Division
Donald J. Crump, *Director*
Philip B. Silcott, *Associate Director*
William L. Allen, William R. Gray, *Assistant Directors*

Staff for this book
Jane H. Buxton, *Managing Editor*
Bonnie S. Lawrence, *Picture Editor*
Marianne R. Koszorus, *Art Director*
Gail N. Hawkins, *Researcher*
Carol A. Rocheleau, *Illustrations Assistant*
Nancy F. Berry, Pamela A. Black, Mary Elizabeth Davis, Rosamund Garner, Victoria D. Garrett, Rebecca Bittle Johns,
Virginia A. McCoy, Cleo E. Petroff, Tammy Presley, Sheryl A. Prohovich, Kathleen T. Shea, *Staff Assistants*

Engraving, Printing, and Product Manufacture
Robert W. Messer, *Manager;* George V. White, *Production Manager*
Mary A. Bennett, *Production Project Manager;* Mark R. Dunlevy, Richard A. McClure, David V. Showers, Gregory Storer, *Assistant*
Production Managers; Katherine H. Donohue, *Senior Production Assistant;* Julia F. Warner, *Production Staff Assistant*

Consultants
Dr. Glenn O. Blough, Peter L. Munroe, *Educational Consultants;* Lynda Ehrlich, *Reading Consultant;* Dr. Nicholas J. Long, *Consulting*
Psychologist; Dr. Gregory Florant, Assistant Professor of Biology, Swarthmore College; Dr. Alfred Gardner, Wildlife Biologist,
U. S. Fish and Wildlife Service; Dr. Valerius Geist, Professor of Environmental Science, University of Calgary; Dr. Roy McDiarmid,
Curator-Research Zoologist, Division of Reptiles and Amphibians, U. S. Fish and Wildlife Service; Dr. Samuel H. Ridgway, Marine
Mammal Researcher, Naval Oceans Systems Center; Dr. Edward S. Ross, Curator of Entomology, California Academy of Sciences;
Dr. George Watson, Curator of Birds, Smithsonian Institution, *Scientific Consultants*

Illustrations Credits
Jen and Des Bartlett (cover); Alan Root/SURVIVAL ANGLIA LTD. (front and back endsheets); Leonard Lee Rue III/THE IMAGE BANK (1); Stephen
J. Krasemann/PETER ARNOLD, INC. (2-3); Bill Ivy (4, 25 right); Leonard Lee Rue III/BRUCE COLEMAN, INC. (5 upper); Steve Maslowski (5 lower);
Stephen J. Krasemann/DRK PHOTO (6 upper); Fred Bruemmer (6 lower); Tom Bledsoe/PHOTO RESEARCHERS, INC. (7); C. Allan Morgan (8-9); Fred
Bavendam (10 lower); Jeff Foott (10-11, 29 center); Bruce Coleman/BRUCE COLEMAN, INC. (11 lower); Laurence Gould/OXFORD SCIENTIFIC FILMS
LTD. (12 upper left); Runk/Schoenberger/GRANT HEILMAN (12 upper right); David Doubilet (12-13); M. P. Kahl, Jr. (14-15, 30-31 lower); Leonard Lee
Rue III/PHOTO RESEARCHERS, INC./NATIONAL AUDUBON SOCIETY COLLECTION (16 upper); ANIMALS ANIMALS/Lynn M. Stone (16 lower);
ANIMALS ANIMALS/Zig Leszczynski (17); E. R. Degginger (18); Stanley Breeden (19 upper); Mike Price/BRUCE COLEMAN, LTD. (19 lower); Lynn
Rogers (20 left, 20-21); Leonard Lee Rue III (22-23); MANTIS WILDLIFE FILMS (23 upper, 23 lower); Edward S. Ross (24 upper, 24 lower, 24-25); Tom
Brakefield (26-27, 29 lower left); Jim Brandenburg (27 upper, 27 lower); Bill McRae (28-29); Dieter Blum/PETER ARNOLD, INC. (30-31); Lynn M.
Stone/BRUCE COLEMAN, LTD. (32).

Library of Congress CIP Data
McCauley, Jane R., 1947-
    Ways animals sleep.

    (Books for young explorers)
    Summary: Describes the different methods of sleep of a variety of mammals, fish, insects, and birds. Includes such details as
postures of sleep, locations, duration, and special adaptation to habitat.
    1. Sleep—Juvenile literature. 2. Animal behavior—Juvenile literature. [1. Sleep. 2. Animals—Habits and behavior] I.
Title. II. Series.
QP425.M39 1983   591.5'1   83-13189
ISBN 0-87044-489-1 (regular edition)
ISBN 0-87044-494-8 (library edition)

A rhinoceros stretches out in
the mud. The mud helps protect
the rhino's skin from the hot sun.
Mud also helps keep insects away.

Cover: A lioness sleeps safely in
the open grassland. Large animals
will not go near her, but flies or ticks
may disturb her rest.

Inside front and back cover: A hippopotamus
props its huge head on another's back.
Hippos often use each other for pillows
as they sleep standing in the water.